TRANSLATIONS ON WAKING IN AN ITALIAN CEMETERY

When Michael Keenan brings you to an Italian cemetery, you realize you need something... And you realize all too quickly that his poems are casting spells, that his whispers and songs and incantations are messing with your dreams, and they enchant and enforce. Keenan is a poet between memory and desire, a poet who sees and makes others want to have seen... I love these poems.

— Ilya Kaminsky
author of *Dancing in Odessa*

Michael Keenan understands, beautifully, that every landscape--urban, rural, pastoral and apocalyptic--is a form of expectation, a pause in earth itself, prepared for splendid display. Worlds move very quickly through these poems, yet every one of them leaves a myth, a wraith of supernumerous being, here with us.

— Donald Revell
author of *Pennyweight Windows: New & Selected Poems*

Michael Keenan's poems illuminate that 'other world, inside this one.' Wearing line breaks to score your heart beat by, these poems limn the phantasmagoric backstreets till dawn, never settling for the comfort of the nihilist's pose. "Etched, fragrant, dark" his sound is original and played with a cutthroat dreamer's intensity. Listen for the shiver, look out for the shiv.

— John Duvernoy
author of *Something in the way// Obstruction Blues*

TRANSLATIONS ON WAKING IN AN ITALIAN CEMETERY

Michael Keenan

© A-Minor Press
www.aminorpress.com

Acknowledgements

Thank you to the editors of the following publications in which some of the poems from this collection have previously appeared: *Posit, the PEN Poetry Series, Fence, Alice Blue Review, Blue Fifth Review, Arsenic Lobster, Shampoo, Redactions, Chronopolis, Flag + Void, Noo Weekly, and Stone Highway Review.* And an overwhelming thank you to A-Minor Press and Nicolette Wong for making this collection a reality.

Cover Picture: Eryk Wenziak
Design & Layout: Walter Bjorkman

Copyright: ©2014 Michael Keenan

ISBN: 978-0692217290 (A-Minor Press)

First Edition A-Minor Press

THE GUERMANTES WAY

DREAMS IN THE WITCH HOUSE, SWANN POINT	17
A BLANK PAGE: IN A BOOK OF BLANK PAGES	18
THE GUERMANTES WAY	19
BATHHOUSE OF THE WINDS	20
THE SEVENTH FLOOR	21
HY BRASIL FOR *THE MISSISSIPPI RIVER'S LAST POET IN RESIDENCE*	22
BALLERINA ON 11th AND NIGHT	24
CRIME JAZZ FOR MEN WITHOUT WOMEN	25
BEARDED MAN WITH HAND OVER HIS HEART	26
TRANSCRIPTED FROM THREE PARTIALLY BURNED PAGES OF *THE BLACK CHRONICLES*	27
ON THE MIDNIGHT SHUTTLE TO THE AIR FRANCE TERMINAL	28
THE MURDERED HARPIST	29
PAULA'S SONG	30
TRANSLATIONS ON WAKING IN AN ITALIAN CEMETERY	31

IN THE ROSE WALL	32
DRIVING ALONE THROUGH THE TED BERRIGAN CEMETERY	34
SPEAKING OF MIRACLES	35
TRANSLATIONS ON WAKING IN AN ITALIAN CEMETERY	36
EVERYTHING I DID I DID OUT OF FEAR	37
TRANSLATIONS ON WAKING IN AN ITALIAN CEMETERY	38
LIGHT THE DEAD SEA	39
BEAUTY IN A LEATHER JACKET	40
TRANSLATIONS ON WAKING IN AN ITALIAN CEMETERY	41
STRAWBERRY WELL	42
BATHHOUSE OF THE WINDS	43
ON PURCHASING A CRYSTAL MONACLE IN THEBES	44
CHURCH OF THE RED MUSEUM	45
ON SPYING HARPIES OVER *KARLUV MOST*	46
MINSTREL SHOW OF THE WASTED YEAR, I WILL REMEMBER YOU ALIVE	47
SONG OF A MAN WHO HAS COME THROUGH DREAM CARS	48

BROOKLYN MUSUEM

A SONG FOR THE FONES ALLEY HUSTLERS	51
A SONG FOR DELICATE SPIDERS	52
BROOKLYN MOON	53
MORNINGSIDE BLUES	54
BROOKLYN MUSEUM	55
BROOKLYN EVENING	56
BLACK CHRISTMAS	57
FOUND IN THE CAPTAIN'S LOG OF *THE ELKA GLORY*	58
VICTORIA'S WINTER	59
AFTER THE DRIVING POEMS	60
TO THE STATUE OF A WITCH WITH FLOWING STONE HAIR WHO WAITS FOR US EVEN NOW	61
THE GIRL WITH THE BANNER GRACEFULLY MARCHES TOWARDS THE BURNING POLICE CAR	62
THE LIGHTNING SONATA	63
TWO LINES ON THE BROOKLYN FIRE	64

THE KHYBER PASS   65

WRITTEN IN THE MARGINS OF *THE BOOK
OF JAGUAR PRIESTS*   66

A. PROVENZANO LANZA FUNERAL HOME INC.   67

MORNINGSIDE BLUES   68

GREENWOOD CEMETERY   69

DRIVING TO NEW ORLEANS, LOUISIANA

SONG FOR A FRAGILE PAINTING	73
CHURCHYARD BLUES	74
DRIVING TO NEW ORLEANS, LOUISIANA	75
ON THE RAILROAD BRIDGE AFTER READING FRANK STANFORD TO THE PASSING KAYAKERS OF DEATH	76
VIRGINIA REEL	77
THE ABANDONED FUNERAL HOME	78
STILL LIFE OF COFFEE FACTORY, TO THE TUNE "SUMMER, 1862"	79
THE GUERMANTES WAY	80
HAUNTED HOTEL ON URSULINES	81
A WHITE NIGHT: IN A BOOK OF WHITE NIGHTS	82
LAST SUMMER IN HELL	83
CRYSTAL STAIR	84
FROM *OLNEY HYMNS*	85
FOUND IN THE CAPTAIN'S LOG OF *THE ELKA GLORY*	86
AFTER RIMBAUD ON THE MOONWALK	87

TRANSLATIONS ON WAKING IN AN
ITALIAN CEMETERY   88

ON CATCHING *THE CHUPACABRA BLUES*   89

CAFÉ DU MONDE'S POET IN RESIDENCE FALLS ASLEEP
WITH ONE OF HIS NOTEBOOKS OPEN   90

DUSK LITANY   91

THE GUERMANTES WAY

DREAMS IN THE WITCH HOUSE, SWANN POINT

Maple blossoms for Lotte

and a tyrant snow

I left that night
because I

had a horrible
dark

      feeling, there

was nothing there
for me, nothing

left, nothing
to begin

         with 10 months in the mirror, watching you/fade

I needed something

    A pine-forest-frenzy, coming
    full-on-night

A mirrorball
macabre, no more
snow,

All
the crosses in Greenville

A blank page: in a book of blank pages.

A BLANK PAGE: IN A BOOK OF BLANK PAGES

THE GUERMANTES WAY

Cigarettes,
check. Places to
go

check.

BATHHOUSE OF THE WINDS

      Held up
      too, to the
      light

      In a pear: Paula's

      lime garden, Mirabai's scythe, bail
bondsmen
        dreaming in neon.

            Regardless, the moon.

Regardless,
sparrows

lifting brilliant black buoys
of cars driving by

Blanca will come.

THE SEVENTH FLOOR

Guitars stacked on

books,

mountains,

the color of vomit,

        Misery's moon,

    Lookout
    point

An ambulance drifts in

to a snowbank.

HY BRASIL FOR *THE MISSISSIPPI RIVER'S LAST POET IN RESIDENCE*

These nights I only

meet girls in hospitals and hospital

waiting

rooms, watching a

sunset or

two

with the silence of

someone

is happy out

there, I'm sure of it, may

they have store-bought lemonade

and extra days off

work, polished mausoleums and beach/black

eyes. This

city has it in for me,

you

know, and this street. If I ever make it

out of here, if you ever make it,

Hallways, green

ones, are the ones that hurt, I wanted to trust

Anna, but did she even remember?

BALLERINA ON 11th AND NIGHT

Red-hair-homily.

Lit window

of the loneliest

walk,

whose brightest city will help me

breathe

the Autumn like the others? The

fight was Halloween night. I have learned. I

have payed. Help me

to run the dark again. Real,

and in the water of a dove-light killing, driving

delirious through the canyon between Boulder and Denver, Cabira

and Bodhgaya, into every all-night-diner.

CRIME JAZZ FOR MEN WITHOUT WOMEN

Two girls on
one street, one
drive from Boulder,
Colorado

      to Shitfuck, Wherever,

Ballerina, meet me

In the elm.

BEARDED MAN WITH HAND OVER HIS HEART

Rappucini's Daughter's June
Garden Glow

    Poison, you
    know

Poison

TRANSCRIPTED
FROM THREE PARTIALLY
BURNED
PAGES OF *THE
BLACK CHRONICLES*

Crawling

Across the state line, baffled,

Sick, lights,
dark

THE MURDERED HARPIST

for J.D. Salinger

Do you remember when we broke the bed, she
says, I wrap the book

around my heart, I
was 18, imagining flowers
pouring
out from it, it being the walk
from one room to
the night, the night's room now, and then.

ON THE MIDNIGHT SHUTTLE TO THE AIR FRANCE TERMINAL

Nursing her honey
suckle
heart, alive
in blue vapors, it

was only myself, unlit
alone

            Again, only myself calming my

      Self, terror that the new life is.

PAULA'S SONG

Only
sometimes she haunts,

not as black smoke and not as black
rain, and never as
a nurse lifting
chartreuse ribbons
from

A graveyard sewer.

TRANSLATIONS ON WAKING IN AN ITALIAN CEMETERY

A crow's corsage, pulling
over

to vomit, a
childhood alone,
but

not alone at all, the
beautiful

undertaker
smokes a damp

cigarette
behind a glass

mausoleum, whispers
to you

with a green
heart in a green

blanket about a mystical
storm drain

where you'll find her

forever, I'll
write to

the graveyard snow.

IN THE ROSE WALL

I was always seeking

out radio towers from Paula's window

from

the roof with Tim my

first friend it goes on

and on nothing

more than a

dream there are new

shadows

new music the Autumn is

listening Tim my

first friend climbing

the light wet with the moon *we*

had all moved away

*There was music all
night*

It was after 2 AM it

was getting later

DRIVING ALONE THROUGH THE TED BERRIGAN CEMETERY

Prague alive, my
parents

and a girl, it
was October, there

were blue rose
bushes or should have
been

Ballerina, I have
danced

SPEAKING OF MIRACLES

Pretty girl on *The
Chapin*

Street Ghost Tour, you
either die or
you

Don't, I
am lost in a picture

of a washed-out pathway, laid
smooth

For two shadows, one
of them will/be me.

TRANSLATIONS ON WAKING IN AN ITALIAN CEMETERY

Years of shyness, covered
by two clouds.

      As devoted gardens,

The red bridge/waits: *heartbroken*

sweaters
wound with dusk.

EVERYTHING I DID I DID OUT OF FEAR

The worlds wear away and return
as rain

       As dignified knocking on

all the wrong doors—

Unseen bird in simple flight: etched,
fragrant, dark.

TRANSLATIONS

ON WAKING

IN AN ITALIAN

CEMETERY

Two letters to Victoria, alone

on the table, I

touch

Them, quickly, *Brooklyn*

Museum

LIGHT THE DEAD SEA

for Frank Stanford

My ghost-ship taken from me,
And I don't even get to die.
Who will ride off in
To the sunset this time? I
do not think it will be me.

BEAUTY IN A LEATHER JACKET

A woman in love with
the golem, no
legend, the real
one, waiting around in
an open coffin, singing
like Paula before her, she
leaps into the crystal Mississippi,
sweeps her arm
towards

The prison, the parachute, my

Shore-leave just ending on blueberry hill.

TRANSLATIONS ON WAKING IN AN ITALIAN CEMETERY

        Infrared afternoon,

        Only a river, a washed-up

        river-bride—

        Sparrow, I whisper this to Kriti.

STRAWBERRY WELL

A passing fire, Paula's
cold song circles a
revolver, a
diary

A dead man, face down, in

A painting of a pool.

BATHHOUSE OF THE WINDS

Spiral staircase
to

a few
more daylights,

isn't so much to
ask

ON PURCHASING A CRYSTAL MONOCLE IN THEBES

Rifling
through miracles, I

found you sweatered
and upstairs in

The spiral stacks: June 2nd

        still a mystery, an
    underground noon,

The dream we all had/when we were alive.

CHURCH OF THE RED MUSEUM

It's a passing story, held
up too
to a
talisman
or shadow, touching
the earth at the
knees 90
years ago, the summer
rain in contact with everyone—

Someone should stay
awake.

ON SPYING HARPIES OVER *KARLUV MOST*

Oh, my fire, friend
of the lost

day, return
to me in a song

played
forever on a glass-

    -lute in a glass wind—

        "Locked in a flower, until the flower gives way."

MINSTREL SHOW OF THE WASTED YEAR, I WILL REMEMBER YOU ALIVE

No ships today

Dumb geese, phosphorescence

Milk
weed, milk-torch,

running down into the branches
with someone

I can never see, but rumors
of a summer-life

      by the diamond-side

           together, daylight or rain, drowsing

                at wonder,

Everything with apple butter and a film-noir-flame

Carlos Lara says: We should have driven further/It is always

           Night/Two and Two

        Girls make love.

SONG OF A MAN WHO HAS COME THROUGH DREAM

CARS

One more rung, in
the full-beard neon, in
the crime,

of Laurel's hair.
One more rung
to dance like wind
on, the roofers watching
behind two castles, we
see

The Pacific Ocean, we
do, in one/perfect/line

       from my hearse to yours, but

First, the black art.

BROOKLYN MUSUEM

A SONG FOR THE FONES ALLEY HUSTLERS

John
Keats, let's
go
walking

where the girls are, Doctor
Johnson, you

come, too. No
logic but that of a cool
night

grave, *mystical*

gun, for
hire

A SONG FOR DELICATE SPIDERS

      Anar, safely
      quiet in

her room, one
sheet

            over the window barely
      open, so quiet, the

moon left ajar—

Tennessee, catapults, kissers in
the bar, I
was one, I was, no
one will

Believe me, but I was
with a beautiful
woman and a friend from
back

Home, to the left of the wind, inside the last dark.

BROOKLYN MOON

Myself, driving
over the George Washington
bridge

Sparkling graffiti *of*
her rooftop trellis

Softly, music, water
from a dove

Two butterflies
drinking the night sky

MORNINGSIDE BLUES

I'll just have to live frugal, and
freezing.

One streetlight is enough, an
unlimited white cloak

for the window, three
years in a trashcan nearly

through West Fourth Street, two
papaya dogs and a lover's

walk, everyone inside dreaming
the inside. Even

the snow has such
small wings.

BROOKLYN MUSEUM

I will insert your
letter where
it says *for*
night

beneath my
windows and curtains, my

flower
pot of broken

glass,
suddenly

how softly the winter
comes

on, Bob's
window three

flights up, Mad's
painting

shining out in
to the concrete
garden, our
home, it
was

    All as clear and certain as parking illegally

On Court Street in the middle of the day.

BROOKLYN EVENING

Alison's there, a wind in
blue, so

sad, soft, lips
lifting

what New
England song, sleeping

for free, my
brother

and I,
the

clouds, the
window, open

finally, like
bread stealing

birds for the witch/black moon.

BLACK CHRISTMAS

Evrium lights two cigarettes, one
for herself and one
for Sleazy
Josh who touches
Amber as he watches us
watch Esre waltz
across the
room

A dark, blue waltz we all
recognize as death

FOUND IN THE CAPTAIN'S LOG OF *THE ELKA GLORY*

There is beauty
here, but

at what cost, Veronica's

    Veil salutes the black train.

Carlos, is there time?

VICTORIA'S WINTER

        Familiar breath-
        -chains, open, sudden-

                -ly slipping off your glass heart softly:

sun-drenched photographs
taking themselves

AFTER THE DRIVING POEMS

I remember smoking
off the hotel
balcony
in Germany, the cat I
watched
for what must
have been an hour, prowling, slowly
along the moon-wet
fence. One
Winter.

In fact, is
all I
remember of *the
SS stars*

TO THE STATUE OF A WITCH
WITH FLOWING
STONE HAIR WHO
WAITS FOR US EVEN
NOW

Lights Vienna
Pornography Streets she
answers
the best she/can

THE GIRL WITH THE BANNER
GRACEFULLY
MARCHES TOWARDS
THE BURNING POLICE
CAR

The few of
us pulling her
back,

THE LIGHTNING SONATA

Grand Army Plaza

Whispering
faces

Eastern Parkway

as a telepathic
tendril

A feather, as
snow, snow-roses rise
from

        her condemned lunar

calendar, and sky.

TWO LINES ON THE BROOKLYN FIRE

rain in a girl, sub-
-way, sun-lit

THE KHYBER PASS

Change is
life, the waitress
tells

me years
later in a new

café two
stops down from the

old one. One
friend.

Is all I know
of snow *is*

the color of my true love's hair.

WRITTEN IN THE MARGINS OF *THE BOOK OF JAGUAR PRIESTS*

Goodbye, solar
subway

8:12

00:00

Brooklyn Museum.

Brooklyn
Moon.

Love in dark clothes, understood
as that

and nothing
more mystical

Understood, as dark love

Driving in
to the poem

you came back to write alone

A. PROVENZANO LANZA FUNERAL HOME INC.

Not being cold
anymore, but not being
warm

                Blaire's body

      I wrote today

for no particular

reason

MORNINGSIDE BLUES

One street

      light of my rose-
      -white

      darkness, 6A

      M: burying

      trees

GREENWOOD CEMETERY

And then I knew
how to end the poem.

Her Carolina
hands, my washed
up Manderley

of ravens cloaking Hell, I
know Music

Darkness: 6 AM

DRIVING TO NEW ORLEANS, LOUISIANA

SONG FOR A FRAGILE PAINTING

The secret dock, closed
tonight, a wild-fire, open, part-moon, part-
                                   -sky.

Nothing
much to see at the coffin

shop today, save
for this crow

In a field of crows

CHURCHYARD BLUES

The first time, I
didn't speak, this time,
a rancor of wind-

-blown owls sear The Mississippi Gloom

I roll over and a penny falls off me, the year 1986

It was a simple day

*Through a park and all London, she
didn't ask me to come*

A simple day, she
didn't ask me to come.

DRIVING TO NEW ORLEANS, LOUISIANA

When a black star walks under a white ladder no one sees anything wrong, but when the opposite happens you'll agree that it's night and you will be afraid.
                                               Andre Breton

I wish it was Nicole who
broke my heart, spending all my
money

on beignets, coffee, sunlight, I
went to kiss her

In the dream, and she
moves her

mouth towards what I suddenly
know

Is the last midnight flower to ever bloom in the graveyard out

                                                                     the window

           We are standing in an ashen hallway leading to a drawing room

                                              with nothing

In it but two beds and two guitars, a silver-hollow-body

                    Les Paul, and a large jewel-encrusted nine-string,

Also a Les Paul, which I proceed to steal when she walks into the moon.

ON THE RAILROAD BRIDGE AFTER READING FRANK STANFORD TO
THE PASSING KAYAKERS OF
DEATH

There have been many
victories. Quiet,
small, and hidden
in tombs

with secretly-bright estuaries of stars.

    Here, there is
    no poetry.

        We drove

into the moon.

VIRGINIA REEL

All those cigarettes piled

up, our last

late night together.

That's what I was

trying to remember. And

the secret hill

hidden in the prostitute

thicket behind

the funeral home

I used to live above—

Standing there with my

friends, watching the one train

float by in silence, always

in silence, moments like that, that

That's what I was

THE ABANDONED FUNERAL HOME

We each lay in the casket
for as long as
we could
take
it, handle the last dark
alone and all that

So still, Virginia, drunk
on a song

And Logan pretending to disappear forever

STILL LIFE OF COFFEE FACTORY, TO THE TUNE "SUMMER, 1862"

A cup of wind, a cigarette, a

night-sky sun-

      -rise from her railway window,

was all I ever wanted to/say.

THE GUERMANTES WAY

              A train to Brussels, a French
              song, May

              there be moonlight when I a-
                              -wake

In the river of 862 diamond-mirrors

                        Meadowlarks, and a few stars
                        with

              long names, names

     you make up.

   We'll take three footsteps. Aphrodite

will breathe. We'll bring Rimbaud's rib-basket to live on forever.

HAUNTED HOTEL ON URSULINES

Writing all day, Charlie
Parker on drums.

        A hand's

        been waving in

        my mirror

        ever since the night

        that Blanca

    ...Blanca

A WHITE NIGHT: IN A BOOK OF WHITE NIGHTS

LAST SUMMER IN HELL

We'll pick up a couple of beignets
and
catch the sunset off

The Moonwalk *like fire*
for Claudia

Carlos it is time

CRYSTAL STAIR

There's an abandoned car
from Kansas

              behind my apartment on Kerouac Street

    I park behind it, illegally
    hidden

Beneath a honeysuckle

forest, no
one

seems to/mind.

FROM *OLNEY HYMNS*

Starlings, darkness,
are a throne, although the
day

will steal its own
lantern. Sit back,
cut off
another piece of pineapple with
your legendary neon

bowie knife, and
wait in
the window for
the next ship to come. Old
Summer.

A few intimacies on Avenue A, dandelion-
                              -wine

Provencal daughter of
the salt-flats,

trust me.

FOUND IN THE CAPTAIN'S LOG OF *THE ELKA GLORY*

Bly
translating New Life as New Love.

    Okay, Robert. Okay.

AFTER RIMBAUD ON THE MOONWALK

Apartment one

is vacant.

What vanity, to think

my friend and

I could last.

Chartreuse dawn, mystical river, we laugh

at the morning joggers.

What arrogance, to

think

my heart's

summer was an amber crow *in*

an eternal film noir.

TRANSLATIONS ON WAKING IN AN ITALIAN CEMETERY

        Afterwards The Swedish
        Girls

sat with me in McDonalds—

        they laughed and laughed
        when I said I

        would be a

        Poet one day—did I not
        know to not

        tell people this then?

        The orange trees wept
        with our love,

        regardless, and a gypsy in
        the window set

        down her crystal ball,
        even

        Lautreamont can change

ON CATCHING *THE CHUPACABRA BLUES*

                        I would go to California.

        I would write a brittle hymn.

                Down three dark alleys,
                rain in the rain-

                trees, Hell
                is used up, Summer

                Pastoral—

CAFÉ DU MONDE'S POET IN RESIDENCE FALLS ASLEEP WITH ONE OF HIS NOTEBOOKS OPEN

Finally, life
inside

the river,
love

I least suspected
to find my

own
song for

the last river/bride.

DUSK LITANY

Cold scarves, Erika, ready
at a whisper.

I liked being caught in
the rain's parade

In a doorway of milk, in
love

While alternately wandering through Rhode Island cemeteries and obsessively watching *Twin Peaks*, **Michael Keenan** wrote the chapbook, TWO GIRLS, which was released by Say No Press in 2009. Shortly thereafter he received his MFA in Literary Arts from Brown University and moved to New Orleans, Louisiana where he drove a waffle truck around the French Quarter and wrote poems on receipts from Café Du Monde, some of which have appeared in *Poetry International, the PEN Poetry Series, Fence, A-Minor Magazine, RealPoetik, Paul Revere's Horse, Caketrain, Right Hand Pointing, Ad-Hominem Art Review* and *Blue Fifth Review*, among others. Currently Michael spends his days at Columbia University.

www.ingramcontent.com/pod-product-compliance
Lightning Source LLC
Chambersburg PA
CBHW060211050426
42446CB00013B/3046